"Rising Above: Navigating Life's Challenges with Strength and Purpose"

Title "Rising Above: Navigating Life's Challenges with Strength and Purpose"
Author: Anthony Hingle III
Copyright © 2024 by Anthony Hingle III

About the Author

As the author of "Rising Above: Navigating Life's Challenges with Strength and Purpose," I'm a passionate advocate for youth empowerment and a guiding light for those seeking to overcome the hurdles of poverty. Growing up in an African American community marked by economic challenges, I have experienced firsthand the impact of poverty and the critical role education plays in breaking free from its constraints.

Driven by a deep-seated commitment to uplift the next generation, I embarked on a journey of exploration and understanding. Recognizing that many young lives are veering off course through a series of detrimental decisions, I delved into the complexities that underlie these choices. This exploration was not just an academic exercise but a personal mission, fueled by the belief that insight into these intricate dynamics is crucial for charting a positive course forward.

The creation of "Rising Above" is the culmination of this journey. It's a rich tapestry woven from personal experiences, touching stories, and practical strategies. The book stands as a beacon of hope and empowerment, offering readers the tools to seize control of their destinies. More than just a literary work, it is a blueprint for personal triumph and community transformation.

My vision extends beyond the pages of the book. Through "Rising Above," there's an aspiration to spark a movement—a call to action for individuals and communities to join hands in breaking the chains that bind our youth. The message is clear: resilience, education, and communal support are powerful forces capable of lifting individuals and communities out of poverty.

With a heart full of gratitude and a spirit fueled by determination, I invite readers to be part of this transformative journey. "Rising Above: Navigating Life's Challenges with Strength and Purpose" is more than a book; it's a rallying cry for empowering our youth and forging a world where every young person can thrive. Join in this noble quest to empower, inspire, and create lasting change.

Disclaimer

This book, "Rising Above: Navigating Life's Challenges with Strength and Purpose," is intended to serve as a guide and a source of inspiration for those seeking to overcome life's challenges, particularly for African American teenagers growing up in poverty. It is important for readers to understand that this book does not claim to provide definitive answers or intensive depth on the subjects it covers.

The contents of this book are based on a combination of personal experiences, research, and insights collected from various sources. While every effort has been made to ensure the relevance and helpfulness of the information provided, this book is not a comprehensive manual that addresses all aspects of navigating life's challenges.

The advice and strategies contained herein may not be suitable for every situation. This book is not intended to be a substitute for professional advice, including but not limited to psychological, financial, legal, or educational counseling. Where specific situations require expert guidance, it is recommended that professional services be sought.

This book is designed to point readers in the right direction, offering perspectives and ideas that can be adapted to individual circumstances. It is my hope that readers will use this book as a starting point for further exploration and personal development. The journey of rising above life's challenges is unique to everyone, and this book aims to support that journey, not define it.

TABLE OF CONTENTS

Welcome to "Rising Above: Navigating Life's Challenges with Strength and Purpose," a book dedicated to you. I understand you are growing up in environments marked by poverty and its many challenges. This book is more than just a collection of words; it is a journey, a guide, and a companion in your walk through one of the most transformative phases of your life.

Growing up in poverty is not just a financial state; it's a complex experience that influences your view of the world, your relationships, and your aspirations. It can be a landscape filled with obstacles, but it's also a testament to resilience, creativity, and strength. This book recognizes the weight of these challenges, yet it focuses on the power you hold within to rise above them.

The stories and advice you will find here are not just theoretical. They are rooted in the real experiences of individuals who have walked paths like yours. They have faced the distractions, the pressures, and the doubts that may currently surround you. Through their narratives, you will find echoes of your struggles and, more importantly, blueprints for your triumphs.

We will talk about distractions — those sirens that can lead you away from your goals. These distractions come in many forms: peer pressure, the allure of quick money, the noise of negative influences, and sometimes, the deafening silence of feeling alone in your challenges. Understanding these distractions is the first step toward overcoming them.

But this book is not just about recognizing obstacles; it's about equipping you with the tools to navigate them. Education, often touted as the great equalizer, will be a significant focus. However, we understand that the path to educational achievement is not just about attending school. It's about engaging with learning, understanding its value, and using it as a ladder to climb out of the cycle of poverty.

You'll be invited to look beyond your immediate surroundings and envision a future where you are in control. This is not just about dreaming big; it's about setting tangible goals and making concrete plans to achieve them. It's about building resilience, embracing your identity, and cultivating a positive self-image despite the stereotypes and barriers that might stand in your way.

Financial literacy, an often-overlooked tool in the fight against poverty, will be discussed in depth. You will learn about managing finances, the importance of saving, and ways to make informed decisions about money. This knowledge is power — the power to change your circumstances and to lay a solid foundation for your future.

Your mental and physical well-being are also vital. In these pages, you will find discussions on maintaining health, coping with stress, and addressing mental health challenges. Remember, strength is not just physical; it's also about the resilience of your mind and spirit.

Finally, this book will encourage you to look beyond yourself. You have the potential to be a beacon of hope and a source of positive change in your community. By rising above your circumstances, you can light the way for others to follow.

So, as you turn these pages, remember that this is more than just reading; it's a step towards shaping your future. Your journey is unique, and your story is still being written. Let's begin this journey together, with hope, courage, and the unwavering belief that you can rise above.

Chapter 1: Recognizing Distractions and Staying Focused

"The secret of change is to focus all of your energy, not on fighting the old, but on building the new."
–Socrates

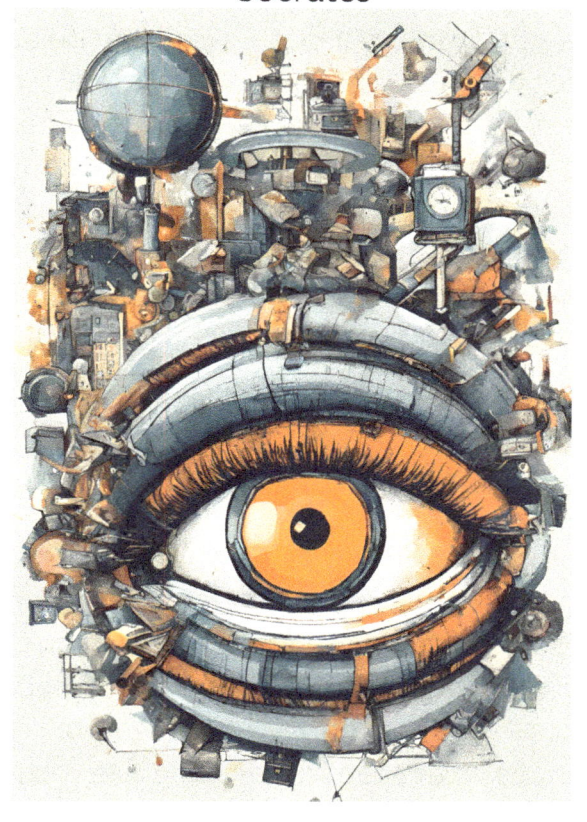

This journey is not just about identifying the hurdles but also about developing the intelligence to navigate through them with your eyes firmly set on your goals.

The Nature of Distractions

Distractions are those elements in your environment that divert you from your path. They can be as obvious as peer pressure and as subtle as self-doubt. Growing up in poverty, these distractions often take on more significant and more tempting forms. The allure of quick money, the escapism offered by substance abuse, the false sense of belonging in a gang, or even the time lost in the vastness of social media can steer you away from your true potential.

Understanding the Impact

The first step in overcoming distractions is understanding their impact. Distractions can lead to a loss of focus, a decline in academic performance, and sometimes, a complete derailment from your life goals. They can cloud your judgment and lead you to make choices that have long-term negative consequences. It's essential to recognize these distractions early and understand the profound impact they can have on your life trajectory.

Strategies to Stay Focused

1. **Set Clear Goals**: Understand what you want to achieve in both the short and long term. These goals should be your anchor, keeping you steady against the waves of distractions.

2. **Develop a Strong Support System**: Surround yourself with people who have your best interests at heart — family members, mentors, teachers, and friends who encourage you to focus on your goals.

3. **Time Management**: Learn to manage your time effectively. Allocate specific hours for studies, recreational activities, and rest. Discipline in your daily routine is a powerful tool against distraction.

4. **Understand the Power of "No"**: Be brave enough to say no to things and people that do not align with your goals. It's a sign of strength, not weakness, to walk away from situations that don't serve your best interests.

5. **Cultivate Self-Awareness**: Regularly assess your actions and decisions. Ask yourself if what you're doing is moving you closer to or further away from your goals.

6. **Seek Inspiration**: Find stories of people who have successfully navigated similar challenges. Let their journeys inspire you to stay focused on your path.

7. Engage in Positive Activities: Participate in activities that enrich you — sports, arts, community service, or learning a new skill. These activities not only keep you engaged but also help in personal growth.

Turning Distractions into Opportunities

Every distraction presents an opportunity to learn and grow. When you choose to focus on your education and goals over a temporary temptation, you build resilience and character. These qualities are invaluable as you navigate through life.

Staying focused in the face of distractions is a skill that will serve you well. It's about making choices every day that align with your goals. Remember, the power to rise above your circumstances lies within you. Your focus, your determination, and your choices will define your journey. Let's continue to build on these strengths as we navigate the chapters ahead, charting a course towards a future filled with hope, achievement, and success.

Chapter 2: Embracing Education as a Pathway Out of Poverty

"Education is the passport to the future, for tomorrow belongs to those who prepare for it today."–Malcolm X

The importance is not just schooling but about embracing learning as a key to unlocking doors to a brighter future.

Education: More Than Just Schooling

Education is often hailed as the great equalizer, and rightly so. However, it's important to distinguish between merely attending school and actively embracing education. True education involves engaging with learning, questioning, exploring, and using knowledge as a tool for personal and community empowerment. It's about understanding that each lesson, each book, and each class is a steppingstone towards changing your circumstances.

The Challenges and How to Overcome Them

The path to educational success is fraught with challenges, more so when poverty adds layers of complexity. Limited resources, underfunded schools, and external pressures can make the journey tough. However, these obstacles are not insurmountable.

1. **Seek Out Resources**: Take advantage of libraries, online courses, tutoring programs, and mentorship opportunities. Many organizations are dedicated to helping students in need.

2. **Create a Learning Environment**: Find or create a space that is conducive to studying. It could be a quiet corner at home, a seat at the public library, or a spot in a community center.

3. **Stay Motivated**: Set educational goals and remind yourself daily why they are important. Visualize where your education can take you.

4. **Build a Supportive Network**: Connect with teachers, counselors, and peers who support your educational aspirations. They can offer guidance, resources, and encouragement.

5. **Utilize Technology Wisely**: Use technology as a tool for learning. Educational apps, online tutorials, and academic forums can be invaluable resources.

Success Stories: Inspiration and Lessons

This chapter would be incomplete without stories of African American individuals who have used education to rise above poverty. These stories not only serve as inspiration but also offer practical lessons and strategies. They show that while the path may be difficult, it is certainly navigable.

African American individuals have historically used education as a powerful tool to rise above poverty and achieve remarkable success in various fields. Here are a few inspiring examples:

1. **Benjamin Carson Sr.** – Born into poverty in Detroit, Benjamin Carson faced numerous challenges, including poor grades and a violent temper. However, his mother encouraged him and his brother to read and pursue education. Carson eventually excelled academically, leading to a full scholarship at Yale University. He became a world-renowned neurosurgeon, best known for his pioneering work in separating conjoined twins.

2. **Oprah Winfrey** – Oprah's early life was marked by poverty and hardship, including being raised in a low-income family in Mississippi. Despite these challenges, she won a scholarship to Tennessee State University. Oprah's persistence and talent in communication and media led her to become one of the most influential media personalities and a philanthropist with a focus on education and empowerment.

3. **John Lewis** – Born to sharecroppers in Alabama, John Lewis was inspired by the civil rights movement to pursue higher education. He attended Fisk University and later the American Baptist Theological Seminary. Lewis became a prominent civil rights leader and a long-serving member of the U.S. Congress, advocating for justice and equality.

4. **Mae Jemison** – grew up in Chicago and developed an early interest in science and space. She excelled in her studies, earning a degree in chemical engineering from Stanford University and a medical degree from Cornell University. Jemison became the first African American woman to travel in space, inspiring many to pursue careers in STEM fields.

These individuals demonstrate the transformative power of education in overcoming poverty and achieving extraordinary success. Their stories are a testament to the resilience, determination, and talent within our community, serving as powerful inspiration for anyone growing up in similar circumstances.

Education Beyond Academics

While academic success is crucial, education in other life skills is equally important. Financial literacy, emotional intelligence, and practical skills like coding or public speaking can open numerous doors. Engage in extracurricular activities that develop these skills.

The Long-Term Perspective

It's vital to view education as a long-term investment in your future. The knowledge and skills you acquire now will pay dividends throughout your life. Whether it's getting into college, securing a good job, or simply being able to navigate the world more effectively, education is your most powerful tool.

In your journey out of poverty, education is your strongest ally. It's more than just a pathway to a career; it's a means to expand your mind, understand the world, and change your circumstances. Embrace every learning opportunity, knowing that each step you take is a step towards a brighter, more empowered future. Let's carry this understanding forward as we explore the next chapters, building on the foundation that education provides.

Chapter 3: Building a Supportive Community

"Alone, we can do so little; together, we can do so much."
—Helen Keller

Community plays a critical role in the lives of teenagers. Building and being part of a supportive community can provide strength, guidance, and opportunities that are essential for overcoming life's challenges.

The Power of Community

A supportive community can be a source of emotional support, practical assistance, and invaluable resources. It can be a safe haven, a place of learning, and a space where you can be understood and empowered. It's where mentors, role models, peers, and even adversaries teach you valuable life lessons.

Finding Your Community

1. **Family and Extended Relatives**: Your immediate and extended family can be a strong support system. They provide a sense of belonging and understanding of your roots and identity.

2. **Schools and Educational Institutions**: Schools are more than just places of learning. They are communities where you can find mentors, join clubs, and engage with peers who share your interests and challenges.

3. **Local Organizations and Clubs**: Participating in local organizations, sports teams, clubs, or groups focused on arts, technology, or community service can open doors to new friendships and opportunities.

4. Faith-Based Groups: Many find a sense of community and support in faith-based groups, which often offer a range of programs and support for young people.

5. **Online Communities**: Digital platforms can connect you with supportive networks worldwide, offering a space to share experiences, learn, and find mentorship.

The Role of Mentors

Mentors play a crucial role in guiding and shaping your path. They can offer advice, share their experiences, and open doors to opportunities that might otherwise be inaccessible. Seek out mentors who inspire you – teachers, community leaders, or professionals in fields you are interested in.

Giving Back to Your Community

While receiving support from your community is essential, actively contributing to it is equally important. Volunteering, mentoring younger children, or participating in community projects not only enriches your community but also fosters your personal growth and sense of purpose.

Overcoming Negative Influences

Every community has its share of negative influences and challenges. Learning to navigate these, to differentiate between constructive and destructive influences, is a critical skill. Surround yourself with people who uplift you and steer clear of those who pull you down.

Building a Diverse and Inclusive Community

Embrace diversity in your community. Engaging with people from different backgrounds, cultures, and experiences broadens your perspective, fosters empathy, and prepares you for a global society.

Your community shapes who you are and who you become. It provides a foundation of support, learning, and growth. In the next chapters, we will build on this concept, exploring how you can leverage your community to overcome obstacles and achieve your goals. Remember, a strong community not only supports your journey but also celebrates your successes and stands with you during challenges.

Chapter 4: Financial Literacy and Empowerment

"An investment in knowledge pays the best interest."
–Benjamin Franklin

Financial literacy is an essential yet often overlooked aspect of empowerment for teenagers, particularly those in poverty. This chapter aims to equip you with the knowledge and skills to make informed financial decisions, an empowerment tool that can significantly impact your life's trajectory.

Understanding Financial Literacy

Financial literacy is more than just understanding money; it's about mastering the skills and knowledge required to manage financial resources effectively. This includes budgeting, saving, investing, and understanding credit. For those growing up in poverty, these skills are vital in breaking the cycle of financial struggle and achieving long-term security and prosperity.

The Basics of Budgeting

Budgeting is the cornerstone of financial literacy. It's about understanding your income, managing your expenses, and planning for both short-term needs and long-term goals. Learning to budget effectively can help you stretch limited resources and make informed spending decisions.

1. **Track Your Income and Expenses**: Start by tracking how much money comes in and where it goes. This awareness is the first step in taking control of your finances.

2. Prioritize Your Spending: Learn to differentiate between needs and wants. Prioritize essential expenses and find ways to reduce non-essential spending.

3. **Set Financial Goals**: Whether it's saving for college, a special purchase, or just a rainy-day fund, setting clear financial goals can help you stay focused and motivated.

The Importance of Saving

Saving money is crucial, no matter how small the amount. It's about creating a financial cushion that can help you in times of emergency and enable you to take advantage of opportunities when they arise.

1. **Start Small**: Even a few dollars saved regularly can add up over time.

2. **Use a Savings Account**: Consider opening a savings account, if possible, where your money can earn interest.

Understanding Credit

Credit can be a double-edged sword. Used wisely, it can help you make significant purchases and build a credit history. However, mismanaged credit can lead to debt and financial challenges.

1. **Learn About Interest Rates and Fees**: Understand how interest rates work and the costs associated with borrowing money.

2. **Use Credit Responsibly**: If you have access to credit, use it responsibly. Avoid overspending and pay your bills on time.

Investing in Your Future

Investing may seem like a distant concept, but it's never too early to learn about it. Understanding the basics of investing can provide you with another tool to build wealth over time.

1. **Learn the Basics**: Start with understanding simple investment concepts and how they can help your money grow over the long term.

2. **Seek Knowledge**: Utilize resources like books, online courses, and financial workshops to learn more about investing.

Goal Example: Create and Maintain a Personal Budget

Objective: The aim is to develop an understanding of personal finances and the importance of budgeting. This goal will help you gain control over your spending, save money, and plan for future expenses.

Steps to Achieve the Goal:

1. **Understanding Income and Expense**s:
   - Begin by tracking all sources of income, such as allowances, part-time job earnings, or gifts.
   - List all your regular expenses, including both necessities (like food, transportation) and discretionary spending (like entertainment, hobbies).

2. **Creating the Budget:**
   - Use a simple spreadsheet or budgeting app to allocate your income towards your expenses.
   - Prioritize necessary expenses and think critically about where you can reduce spending.

3. **Setting Savings Goals:**
   - Decide on a percentage or amount of your income to save each month. Even a small amount consistently saved can grow over time.
   - Set specific savings goals (like saving for a new phone, college fund, or a car) to stay motivated.

4. **Monitoring and Adjusting:**
   - Regularly review your budget to ensure you're staying on track.
   - Adjust your budget as necessary if your income or expenses change.

5. **Learning and Growing:**
   - Spend time each month learning about a new financial topic, such as interest rates, investments, or credit scores.
   - Consider joining a financial literacy workshop or webinar.

Reflection and Tracking:
- At the end of each month, reflect on your budgeting process. What worked well? What challenges did you face?
- Keep a journal entry of your savings progress and any new financial insights you've gained.

Outcome:
By the end of this exercise, you should have a clearer understanding of your personal finances, be in the habit of budgeting and saving, and feel more empowered to make informed financial decisions. This goal is not just about managing money, but about building a foundation for financial independence and security.

Financial literacy is a powerful tool in your arsenal as you navigate out of poverty and towards your goals. It is about making informed choices, understanding the value of money, and planning for the future. As we move to the next chapters, keep in mind that financial empowerment is a crucial step in taking control of your life and carving out a path to success and stability.

Chapter 5: Overcoming Adversity with Resilience

"The oak fought the wind and was broken, the willow bent when it must and survived."
—Robert Jordan

Resilience is a crucial quality for success and personal growth. This chapter explores the nature of adversity, the importance of resilience, and practical ways to cultivate this invaluable trait.

Understanding Resilience

Resilience is the ability to bounce back from setbacks, adapt to challenging circumstances, and keep moving forward in the face of adversity. It's not about avoiding difficulties but learning how to navigate through them and emerge stronger. Resilience is particularly crucial for many of us growing up in poverty, where challenges can be frequent and overwhelming.

The Role of Adversity

Adversity comes in many forms: financial hardship, discrimination, negative peer pressure, or personal loss. While these experiences can be daunting, they also provide opportunities for growth and learning. Each challenge you overcome builds your resilience, making you better equipped to handle future obstacles.

Building Resilience

1. **Maintain a Positive Outlook**: A positive mindset can be your most powerful tool in facing adversity. It involves recognizing the good in every situation and focusing on solutions rather than problems.

2. Set Realistic Goals: Setting and working towards achievable goals, even small ones, can give you a sense of control and purpose, bolstering your resilience.

3. Develop Problem-Solving Skills: Learn to approach problems with a calm and logical mindset. Break them down into manageable parts and tackle them step by step.

4. Seek Support When Needed: Resilience doesn't mean going at it alone. Seeking help and support from family, friends, mentors, or counselors is a sign of strength, not weakness.

5. Learn from Setbacks: Every setback is a lesson. Reflect on what went wrong, what you learned, and how you can use that knowledge in the future.

6. Take Care of Your Physical and Mental Health: Regular exercise, a healthy diet, adequate sleep, and practices like meditation can strengthen your physical and mental resilience.

The Power of Personal Stories

Incorporating personal stories of individuals who have faced and overcome adversity can provide inspiration and practical examples of resilience in action. These stories can serve as a reminder that challenges can be steppingstones to success.

Growing up in a low-income neighborhood, a young lady faced adversity from a young age. Her community was plagued with crime and a lack of educational resources, and as a young African American girl, she often felt the heavy weight of societal expectations and limitations. Despite these challenges, she was determined to rise above her circumstances. She spent countless nights studying by the dim light in her small room, driven by a dream of becoming a lawyer. With the support of a local mentorship program, she excelled academically and earned a scholarship to a prestigious university. Throughout college, she faced financial struggles and racial discrimination, but she remained steadfast, channeling her experiences into advocacy for those who faced similar challenges. She not only graduated with honors but also returned to her community as a beacon of hope, using her law degree to fight for justice and equality. Her journey serves as a powerful testament to the resilience of the human spirit and a reminder that adversity can indeed be a steppingstone to extraordinary success.

Coping with Discrimination and Injustice

You may face unique challenges like racial discrimination and social injustice. Building resilience in the face of these issues involves staying informed, engaging in constructive dialogue, and advocating for change, all while maintaining your sense of self-worth and dignity.

Resilience is not an innate trait but a skill that can be developed over time. It is about facing life's challenges with courage and determination, learning from each experience, and not letting setbacks define you. As you move forward in your journey, remember that the resilience you build today will be the foundation of your success and happiness in the future. Let's carry this strength into the next chapters, where we will explore more tools to help you rise above your circumstances.

Chapter 6: Health and Wellbeing

"Take care of your body. It's the only place you have to live."
−Jim Rohn

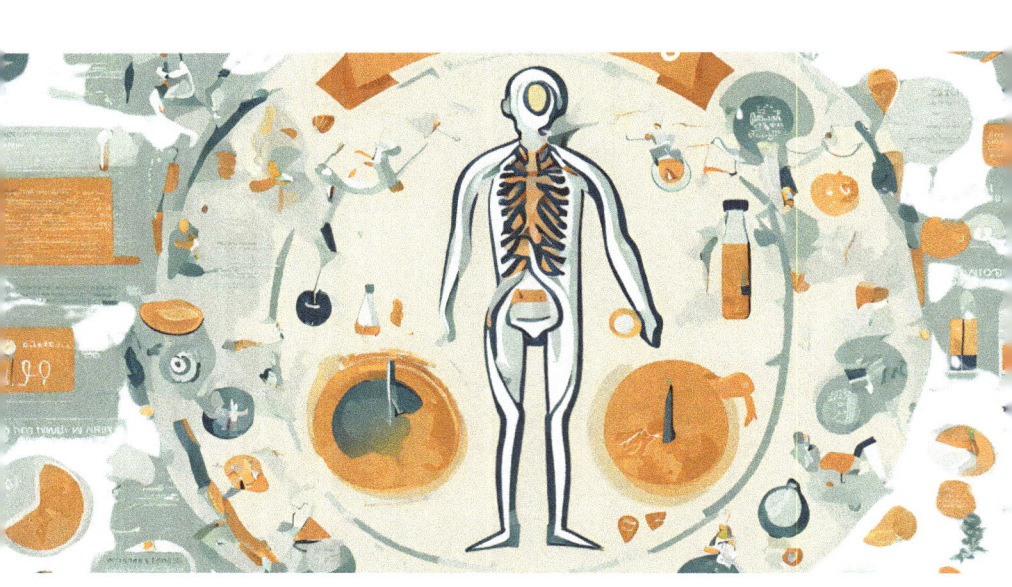

Let's emphasize the critical role of health and wellbeing. This chapter aims to provide insights and practical advice on maintaining both physical and mental health, which are fundamental to achieving success and happiness.

The Importance of Physical Health

Your physical health is the foundation upon which many aspects of your life are built. Good health enables you to pursue your goals with energy and endurance. However, growing up in poverty can often mean limited access to nutritious food, safe recreational spaces, and healthcare.

1. **Nutrition on a Budget**: Learn about affordable, nutritious foods that can maximize health benefits without straining your budget. Community resources like food banks and nutrition programs can be invaluable.

2. **Staying Active**: Regular physical activity is vital. It doesn't have to be expensive gym memberships; walking, jogging, or community sports are great ways to keep fit.

3. **Prioritizing Sleep**: Never underestimate the power of a good night's sleep. Adequate sleep is crucial for your physical and mental health.

4. Preventive Healthcare: Take advantage of community health resources, such as clinics and health fairs, which often offer free or low-cost services.

Mental Health: Breaking the Stigma

Mental health is as important as physical health, yet it often carries a stigma, especially in many African American communities. Recognizing and addressing mental health issues is a sign of strength and a critical step towards overall wellbeing.

1. **Understanding Mental Health**: Educate yourself about the signs and symptoms of mental health issues like depression, anxiety, and stress.

2. **Seeking Help**: If you're struggling, don't hesitate to seek help from counselors, therapists, or trusted adults. Many organizations offer free or low-cost mental health services.

3. **Building Emotional Resilience**: Techniques like mindfulness, meditation, and journaling can help in managing stress and building emotional resilience.

4. **Creating a Support Network**: Surround yourself with people who understand and support your mental health journey.

The Impact of Substance Abuse

Substance abuse is a significant issue in many communities, often exacerbated by poverty and stress. Understanding the risks and long-term effects of substance abuse is crucial.

1. **Education and Awareness**: Educate yourself about the dangers of drugs and alcohol. Knowledge is a powerful tool in making informed choices.

2. Seeking Help for Addiction: If you or someone you know is struggling with addiction, seek help. There are numerous resources and programs available to support recovery.

Goal Example: Establish a Consistent Exercise Routine

Objective: The goal is to foster physical health and mental well-being through regular exercise. This will not only improve your physical fitness but also enhance your mood, energy levels, and overall mental health.

Steps to Achieve the Goal:

1. **Assess Current Fitness Level**:
   - Start by understanding your current physical condition. Consider any health concerns or limitations.
   - Set realistic exercise goals based on your assessment.

2. Choose Enjoyable Activities:
- Select physical activities that you enjoy. This could be anything from jogging, cycling, dancing, to team sports or yoga.
- Enjoying your exercise routine increases the likelihood of sticking to it.

3. Create a Routine:
- Plan specific days and times each week dedicated to exercising. Aim for at least 30 minutes of moderate exercise most days of the week.
- Consistency is key, so try to stick to your schedule as closely as possible.

4. Track Progress:
- Keep a journal or use an app to track your exercise routines, noting the duration and type of activity.
- Celebrate milestones, no matter how small, to stay motivated.

5. Incorporate Mindfulness and Relaxation:
- Include activities that promote relaxation and mindfulness, like yoga or meditation, to enhance mental well-being.
- Pay attention to how your body and mind feel during and after exercising.

6. Seek Support and Accountability:
- Find a workout buddy or join a group to stay motivated.
- Share your goals with friends or family for additional support and accountability.

Reflection and Adjustment:
- Reflect on your exercise routine weekly. What's working well? What challenges are you facing?
- Be flexible and adjust your routine as needed to maintain interest and accommodate any changes in your schedule or lifestyle.

Outcome:
By establishing and maintaining a regular exercise routine, you should experience improvements in physical fitness, mood, and energy levels. This goal is about building a habit that contributes to your overall health and wellbeing, empowering you to lead a healthier, more active lifestyle.

Your health and wellbeing are precious and play a crucial role in your ability to rise above your current circumstances. By taking care of your physical and mental health, you equip yourself to face life's challenges with strength and clarity. Remember that your health is your wealth, a vital asset in your journey towards success and empowerment.

Chapter 7: Setting Goals and Making Plans

"A dream written down with a date becomes a goal. A goal broken down into steps becomes a plan. A plan backed by action makes your dreams come true."
–Greg S. Reid

42

Let's delve into the pivotal role of goal setting and strategic planning in your life. This chapter is a guide to identifying your aspirations, setting achievable goals, and creating actionable plans to turn your dreams into reality.

Understanding the Power of Goals

Goals give direction and purpose to your efforts. They act as beacons, guiding you through the fog of daily distractions and challenges. Setting goals is the first step in a journey towards achievement; it's about knowing where you want to go and what you want to achieve.

Identifying Your Goals

1. **Reflect on Your Passions and Interests**: What excites you? What are you passionate about? Your goals should resonate with your interests and values.

2. **Consider Short-term and Long-term Goals**: Break down your aspirations into short-term (achievable in the next few months to a year) and long-term goals (over a year).

3. **Be Specific and Realistic**: Vague goals are hard to achieve. Make your goals as specific as possible and ensure they are realistic given your current resources and circumstances.

Creating a Roadmap

Once you've set your goals, the next step is to create a roadmap — a detailed plan on how to achieve them. This involves breaking down each goal into smaller, manageable tasks and setting deadlines.

1. **Step-by-Step Approach**: Break down each goal into smaller tasks or steps. This makes the process less overwhelming and easier to manage.

2. **Assign Timelines**: Set deadlines for each task. This creates a sense of urgency and helps keep you on track.

3. **Flexibility**: Be prepared to adjust your plan as circumstances change. Flexibility is key to overcoming unexpected challenges.

Overcoming Obstacles

You will encounter obstacles as you work towards your goals. Anticipating these challenges and having a plan to overcome them is crucial.

1. **Identify Potential Barriers**: Think about what might hinder your progress and plan how to address these challenges.

2. **Seek Support**: Don't hesitate to seek help when faced with obstacles. This could be advice from a mentor, assistance from a friend, or resources from a community program.

3. **Stay Motivated**: Keep your end goal in mind. Remind yourself why these goals are important to you.

Monitoring Progress

Regularly check your progress. Are you on track? Do you need to adjust your plans? This self-review is crucial for staying on course.

1. **Celebrate Small Wins**: Acknowledge and celebrate small achievements along the way. This boosts your morale and keeps you motivated.

2. **Learn from Setbacks**: Instead of being disheartened by setbacks, use them as learning experiences.

SMART Goal Example: Improve Academic Performance in Mathematics

Specific:
- Aim to increase your mathematics grade from a C to a B by the end of the semester.

Measurable:
- Track progress through scores in weekly math quizzes and assignments.
- Schedule a monthly review with your math teacher to discuss improvements and areas needing more focus.

Achievable:
- Dedicate an extra hour each week to study math, focusing on areas of difficulty.
- Utilize online resources and tutoring services for additional support.

Relevant:
- Improving in mathematics is important for your overall academic goals and can open doors to more advanced courses in the future.

Time-Bound:
- Set a deadline for the end of the semester to achieve this goal.
- Break down the goal into weekly and monthly milestones to monitor progress.

Action Plan:
1. **Week 1-2**: Identify specific topics in math that are challenging.
2. **Week 3-4**: Start utilizing online resources and tutorials for these topics.
3. **Week 5-6**: Attend tutoring sessions or study groups to reinforce learning.
4. **Week 7-8**: Assess progress in quizzes; consult with the teacher for feedback.
5. **Week 9-10**: Adjust study strategies based on feedback and quiz results.
6. **Week 11-12**: Review and prepare for end-of-semester exams.
7. **End of Semester**: Evaluate final grade and reflect on the effectiveness of the strategies used.

Regular Check-ins:
- Set weekly reminders to review progress.
- Adjust the study schedule as needed based on weekly and monthly reviews.

Outcome:
By following this SMART goal, you aim to not only improve your math grade but also develop effective study habits and a deeper understanding of the subject. This goal is about taking proactive steps to enhance your academic performance, setting a pattern of success that can be applied to other areas of your life.

Setting goals and making actionable plans is a dynamic process that requires patience, perseverance, and adaptability. By clearly defining what you want to achieve and creating a roadmap to get there, you are laying the groundwork for a successful and fulfilling future. As we move forward, let these goals and plans be your compass, guiding you towards your aspirations.

Chapter 8: Cultivating a Positive Self-Image and Identity

"Our deepest fear is not that we are inadequate. Our deepest fear is that we are powerful beyond measure."
–Marianne Williamson

Let's explore the vital importance of cultivating a positive self-image and a strong sense of identity. This chapter is dedicated to understanding self-worth, embracing your identity, and overcoming societal stereotypes and prejudices.

Understanding Self-Image

Your self-image is how you perceive and value yourself. It's influenced by your experiences, your environment, and the messages you receive from those around you and society at large. A positive self-image is crucial because it affects your confidence, your decisions, and ultimately, the trajectory of your life.

Cultivating Self-Esteem

1. **Acknowledge Your Worth**: Recognize that your value is not determined by your circumstances. You have unique talents, abilities, and potential.

2. **Positive Affirmations**: Practice affirming yourself. Positive affirmations reinforce your worth and help combat negative thoughts.

3. **Celebrate Your Achievements**: No matter how small, celebrate your achievements. This reinforces your sense of accomplishment and capability.

4. Surround Yourself with Positivity: Be around people who uplift you and believe in your potential. Their positive perception of you can reinforce your self-esteem.

Embracing Your Identity

Your identity is a tapestry woven from your background, culture, experiences, and beliefs. Embracing your identity means accepting and taking pride in who you are, including your racial and cultural heritage.

1. **Explore Your History**: Learn about the history and contributions of African Americans. Understanding your heritage can instill a sense of pride and belonging.

2. **Resist Stereotypes**: Challenge and resist stereotypes that attempt to define you in a limiting way. You are not a standing stone but a unique individual with your own story.

3. **Express Yourself**: Find ways to express your identity, whether through art, music, writing, or other forms of expression. This can be a powerful tool for self-discovery and affirmation.

Dealing with Discrimination and Prejudice

Unfortunately, discrimination and prejudice are realities that many African American teenagers face. Learning to deal with these experiences in a healthy way is crucial for maintaining a positive self-image.

1. **Educate Yourself**: Understanding the roots and realities of racism can empower you to respond to it effectively.

2. **Seek Support**: Talk about your experiences with trusted individuals. Sharing can be a way to process and overcome the negative impact of these experiences.

3. **Advocate for Change**: Engage in or support initiatives that promote equality and justice. Being part of the solution can be empowering and affirming.

Envisioning and Achieving Your Future - Rhetorical Exercise

Imagine standing at a crossroads, where one path leads to the future you've always dreamed of. Picture yourself five or ten years from now. What do you see? Be specific in your vision.

Wardrobe: Are you dressed in a sharp suit, ready for a corporate boardroom, or in comfortable attire, reflecting a creative and relaxed lifestyle? Do your clothes symbolize success, comfort, creativity, or perhaps a blend of these?

Job/Career: Envision yourself in your ideal job. Are you leading a team, innovating in technology, inspiring young minds, or perhaps running your own business? What does your daily work involve? Feel the satisfaction of doing work that fulfills you.

Location: Where are you? Are you thriving in the bustling energy of a big city, enjoying the tranquility of the countryside, or perhaps living abroad, immersed in a new culture?

Home: Picture the home you return to each day. Is it a cozy apartment with a skyline view, a peaceful house by the beach, or a vibrant home filled with family laughter? Walk through each room in your mind, feeling the comfort and security it provides.

Car: What car do you drive? Is it a sleek, eco-friendly model, a spacious family vehicle, or perhaps a classic, restored with your own hands? Feel the steering wheel under your fingers, and the sense of freedom as you drive.

Kids and Family: If you see children in your future, imagine their faces. How are you contributing to their growth and happiness? If you envision a life partner, what qualities do they have? Feel the support and love that surrounds you.

Relationships: Consider the friends and community around you. How do your relationships enrich your life? Feel the joy and comfort of meaningful connections.

Now, reverse engineer this vision. What steps do you need to take to make this future a reality? Break down your journey into achievable goals.

-**For your career**: Consider the education, skills, and networking required.
-**For your home and location**: Think about the financial planning and career choices that will get you there.
-**For relationships and family**: Reflect on the personal growth and choices that will foster these bonds.

Remember, every great achievement begins with a vision and is followed by determined action. You have the power to make your dreams a reality. Don't stop, go for it! You got this!

Cultivating a positive self-image and embracing your identity are essential steps towards living a fulfilled and empowered life. They form the foundation upon which you build your dreams and aspirations. As we move forward, remember that who you are is a source of strength, not a limitation. Your identity, coupled with a strong sense of self-worth, will be key drivers in your journey to rise above and achieve your goals.

Chapter 9: Making a Difference in Your Community

"Act as if what you do makes a difference. It does."
—William James

You can make a significant impact in your community. This chapter emphasizes the importance of giving back and being a positive force in your surroundings. It's about transforming not only your life but also the lives of those around you.

Understanding Community Impact

Your community is a tapestry of lives, experiences, and stories. When you contribute positively to your community, you help strengthen this tapestry, creating a more supportive, empowered, and resilient environment for everyone. Making a difference isn't just about grand gestures; it's often the small, consistent acts that have the most lasting impact.

Identifying Ways to Contribute

1. **Volunteer Your Time**: Look for volunteer opportunities in your community. This could be tutoring younger students, helping in a local shelter, or participating in community clean-ups.

2. **Share Your Knowledge and Skills**: Use your talents and skills to benefit others. If you're good at a particular subject, consider offering free tutoring. If you're skilled in a sport or an art form, coach or mentor others who are interested.

3. Be a Role Model: Simply by striving for your own goals and maintaining a positive outlook, you can inspire those around you. Your resilience and determination can motivate others to pursue their aspirations.

4. **Advocate for Positive Change**: If there are issues affecting your community, get involved in advocacy work. This could mean joining or starting initiatives to address community challenges, participating in local politics, or supporting social justice causes.

The Benefits of Community Engagement

Engaging with your community is mutually beneficial. It not only helps those around you but also contributes to your personal growth and development.

1. **Building Connections**: Community involvement helps you build a network of supportive and like-minded individuals.

2. **Developing Skills**: Volunteering and community work can help you develop new skills and gain experiences that are beneficial for personal and professional growth.

3. **Enhancing Your Wellbeing**: Contributing to the welfare of others can be profoundly satisfying and can boost your mental and emotional wellbeing.

4. Creating a Supportive Environment: By contributing positively, you help create a community that can support you and others through challenges.

Overcoming Challenges in Community Work

Community work can be challenging. You might face resource constraints, lack of concern, or resistance to change. Persistence, creativity, and collaboration are key to overcoming these challenges.

Making a difference in your community is about recognizing that you have the power to effect positive change. Your actions, no matter how small, can have a ripple effect, improving not just your life but also the lives of those around you. As you move forward, carry with you the understanding that your contributions to your community are an integral part of your journey to rise above and create a brighter future for yourself and others.

As we end, it's important to reflect on the journey we've embarked upon together. This book, aimed at empowering African American teenagers, especially those facing the adversities of poverty, has been more than a compilation of guidance; it's a testament to your resilience, potential, and the promise of a brighter future.

Embracing Your Story

Each chapter of this book has woven together different aspects of your life – overcoming distractions, valuing education, building community, financial empowerment, resilience, health and wellbeing, goal setting, self-identity, and community contribution. Remember, your story is unique. Embrace it with all its challenges and triumphs, for it shapes who you are and who you will become.

The Power Within You

This journey has highlighted one crucial truth: the power to rise above your circumstances lies within you. Your determination, your hard work, and your choices carve the path to your success. You are not defined by your current situation but by how you respond to it. With each challenge you overcome, you grow stronger and more capable.

A Lifelong Journey

The journey of self-improvement and personal growth is ongoing. There will always be new challenges to face, more goals to achieve, and further heights to reach. Keep learning, keep growing, and keep pushing your boundaries. Your potential is limitless.

Giving Back and Moving Forward

As you rise, remember to extend a hand to those coming up behind you. Your experiences, lessons learned, and successes can inspire and guide others. The journey is not just about individual success but about lifting others as you climb.

Staying Grounded in Your Values

As you navigate the complexities of life, stay grounded in your values. Let integrity, respect, and empathy guide your actions and decisions. These values will be your compass, helping you stay true to yourself and your purpose.

Facing the Future with Hope and Courage

The future may seem uncertain but face it with hope and courage. Believe in your ability to overcome obstacles and seize opportunities. Your journey thus far has equipped you with the tools to navigate whatever lies ahead.

The Promise of Your Dreams

Your dreams are valid, and they are achievable. They are not just fanciful hopes but glimpses of what you can truly accomplish. Hold onto them, work towards them, and watch as they unfold into reality.

As we conclude this book, it's not the end of your journey, but rather a new beginning. A beginning filled with possibilities, challenges, and opportunities. Your path will not always be easy, but it is yours to shape. With each step you take, remember that you are not alone. You are part of a community, a history, and a future that is bright with potential.

Your journey ahead is one of purpose, strength, and rising above. Carry these lessons with you and go forth with the confidence that you have the tools, the strength, and the determination to create a life of success and fulfillment. The world awaits your contributions, your leadership, and your unique story. Rise above and make your mark.

1. Educational Support and Tutoring

-**Khan Academy**: A free online resource offering lessons in various subjects, including math, science, and programming.

-**Coursera and edX**: Platforms providing access to free and low-cost college courses from universities around the world.

2. Mentorship Programs

-**Big Brothers Big Sisters of America**: A program matching youths with adult mentors to provide guidance and support.

-**The Boys & Girls Clubs of America**: Offers after-school programs and mentorship for young people.

3. Career and College Preparation

-**College Board**: Provides resources for SAT preparation and college planning.

-**Year Up**: Offers training and internships to young adults, helping them transition into professional careers.

4. Financial Literacy and Management

-**Jump$tart Coalition**: Offers resources and tools to promote financial literacy among students.

-**MyMoney.gov**: A government website providing financial education resources for young people.

5. Health and Wellness

-**The Steve Fund**: Focuses on the mental health and emotional well-being of young people of color.

-**Teen Mental Health**: Provides resources specifically tailored to the mental health of teenagers.

6. Community Engagement and Leadership

-**NAACP Youth & College Division**: Engages young people in social justice advocacy and leadership development.

-**Urban League Young Professionals**: A network focused on community service and professional development for young African Americans.

7. Legal Rights and Advocacy

-**ACLU Know Your Rights**: A resource for understanding and protecting civil rights.

-**Equal Justice Initiative**: Offers legal support and advocates against racial and economic injustice.

8. Technology and Coding Skills

-**Black Girls Code**: Provides opportunities for young African American girls to learn coding and technology skills.

-**Code.org**: Offers free coding lessons and resources for students.

9. Arts and Culture

-**YoungArts**: Supports young artists through competitions, scholarships, and mentorship.

-**The Scholastic Art & Writing Awards**: Recognizes creative talents among teens and offers scholarships.

10. Sports and Recreation

-**YMCA**: Offers various sports, fitness, and recreational programs for youth.

-**The First Tee**: Provides young people with character-building and life skills lessons through golf.

Thank You

I want to extend my deepest gratitude to each one of you who has joined me through the pages of our shared exploration. Your commitment to understanding the intricate realities of being a teenager in poverty, especially as an African American, and engaging with the challenges faced within our communities, is profoundly admirable.

Your willingness to delve into these crucial discussions marks a significant step toward creating a more empowered generation of young people. Throughout this book, we have journeyed together through various strategies for success, highlighting the incredible power of community and collective action. It is your dedication to breaking free from the cycle of bad decisions and striving for a better future that truly inspires.

I am honored to have shared this path with you, filled with learning, advocacy, and a relentless pursuit of a brighter future for all. Your unwavering support and belief in the importance of empowerment have been the backbone of this endeavor. As we close this chapter, let's carry forward the lessons learned and continue to advocate for and work towards a world where every teenager can rise above and achieve their fullest potential.

Thank you for being an integral part of this journey. Your engagement and support have made all the difference. Let's keep the flame of hope and change burning bright as we move forward together.